Gray's Gone

Alexandria Zimmerman

Presentation by *BookLeaf Publishing*

Web: www.bookleafpub.com

E-mail: info@bookleafpub.com

ISBN: 9789357440660

First edition 2023

Mom, thank you for the many late-night chats on the couch talking about everything (even when I knew you really wanted to sleep). And thank you to each sibling, Peyton, Zach, Kiera, and Landon for being my little lights. Lastly, thanks dad for being there to protect me when I was scared.

Gray's Gone

The Last Thing I See
Watery Dark,
Not quite solid Darkness,
Sinking, sinking, sinking,
It's so cold here.
The water is surrounding me,
Filling my lungs,
Invading what little personal space
I have left.

The Last Think I See
Father crying,
Father yelling,
Father grieving,
The loss,
Of another love.

I'm sorry, father.
I couldn't take the pain anymore.

The water seeps into my eyes.
Lungs,
Filling the holes in my heart.

Why is everyone so afraid of death?

Is it the regret?
Of things left undone,
Unsaid,
Unlived?
Or is the fear,
Of seeing your life flash before your eyes?

My life doesn't flash.
Instead, it glides and flows,
Like the water,
I'm drowning in.
Always changing,
Always flowing
In the same direction,
Neither chronological,
Or sensible,
Just.
Life.

My mother sewing
The holes by brother made,
Climbing that new tree,
He doesn't do that now.

My father drinking,
Washing away any memory,
My mother may have imprinted in his mind.

My brothers fighting,

Laughing,
Crying,
Hugging,
Chittering,
Chasing each other,
Around,
And Around.

My mother's funeral,
My father staring blankly,
At the casket
I don't believe
She's really in.

Everyone knows Angels go to Heaven.

William holding tears back,
Baby Charlie,
He didn't understand,
Kept running toward the coffin,
He wanted to wake her up.

Why,
As I'm dying,
Do I think of her death?

There are stars filling my vision,
Talking amongst one another.
Maybe they're debating,

Whether I deserve,
To float or sink,
Heaven or Hell.

I can't think anymore,
The water invades my brain,
With its murky hold.
"No more thinking,
You think too much, little one."
Whispers the lake.

There is a tale of a lady in the lake.
The one with King Arthur.

"Are you she?"
I whisper in return.

Soft chuckles by Lake,
Tinkling laughs by stars.

"Unfortunately"
Was all she said.
Takes my hands,
My wrists,
Arms,
Shoulders,
Legs, ankles, toes,
My being wrapped in the hold,
Of the Lady of the Lake.

I think once more,
Before Lake takes me home,
Why is everyone so afraid,
Of Death?

No One Tells the Lady's Story

No one tells the lady's story,
Her tale disappeared,
Left in the medieval mystery
Of times past.

Her story drowned by others.
Arthur,
Lancelot,
Guinevere.
Merlin: The one who swore,
He would never leave.

No one tells the lady's story,
No one even knows her name.
As if no one cares,
Cares enough to ask her name.
Invisible to all,
Left to swim the waters of legends.
The lake that built her name.
How insignificant one must be
To be known not by one's name,
But by the meaning of it.

Nimue.

The Lady of the Lake.
Now Keres.
Death spirits.

She drags the lonely,
The forgotten,
The unloved and unspoken of,
Drags them into her waters,
Guiding them to their deaths.

Into a death of terror.
She is the reason.
The reason people fear
It
Death.
Dying.
Leaving life. It.

No one tells the lady's story.
Keres nor Nimue.
One in the same.
Remains untold nonetheless.

Shattered Being

Winter is on my tongue
Shard of glass I wish to spit
Into shards my body splits
I don't remember what shattered me,
I'm just a shattered being,

I want to break those who broke me.
That's wrong, isn't it?

Maybe that'll make it go away,
The pain of shattered glass,
Living glass,
Inside a shattered being.

I Can't Remember

Yesterday's date is today,
I don't remember Tuesday,
I know what I did that day.
It's not the same as a memory.

Sometimes I forget where I live,
Don't recoginize the street,
The surrounding houses.
I'm not pretending,
The remembering piece is missing
I'm only 18.
What happened to me?

Will I remember my parents faces
At 23?
Will I get lost repeatedly?
Forget what I was saying frequently?

What was I doing again?

Letters Lost to Sea Pt 1

Dear The One Who Listens,
I write to you under the safety net of my tree.
It's a wonderful tree,
full of lush indigo heart-shaped leaves,
the soft moss underneath it all
provides something like a pillow.

You must love it as well, yes?
I guess I cannot be so sure of this.
 I don't know you do I?
You read my words,
you get to know me
(you know my favorite tree at least),
but I don't know you.

Maybe it's dangerous to write to you,
but I don't care.
Because you're listening to me
like I've always wanted
you read my words as you're doing right now.
I don't know if you read with an open
or judgemental mind,
but with all my heart I hope it's open.

Open as the ocean on a foggy day,

Fog obscuring everything,
No one knows where it ends,
They see where they think it begins,
But that's not really the case is it?
That's their point of view.

And my point of view:
Your mind is as open as such ocean.

Maybe this won't even reach anyone
but if you're reading this
you're going to be my someone.
I know it in the caverns of my soul.

Soul sounds
so much more like forever than heart,
doesn't it?
Hearts are temporary,
fading and sickening with time,
decomposing when its host is gone.
Souls are infinite in time.
They're the human energy
 that causes nerves to light up with
personality, ambitions,
both love and lust.
Altruicity and greed.
Patience and wrath.
Yes, I am more partial to the soul than the heart.

And more partial to you than the rest.
You're the one
Who listens.

He's Gone, Papa

Little Charlie,
How sweet a name,
Watches his brother,
Wash upon the shore.

Gray's gone,
But how interesting the human mind must be,
For all Charlie thought,
"Why does it have to be so hot?"
How simple children's minds are.
Not knowing death quite yet,
Only knowing that life isn't permanent.

Charlie watches Papa,
Watching Gray.
Papa mumbling,
Papa clutching his hands,
Papa's eyes swollen.
This was wear Charlie's understanding,
Came to an abrupt end.

He had never seen someone so big cry.
Charlie didn't understand.

"What happened to Gray"

"He's gone Charlie."
"Gone?"
"Dead"
Papa cries.
"He's gone, papa".
Charlie hugs.
Papa held him close.

Papa retreats back to the cellar.
And drinks until he drowns too.

Shh, Don't Tell

Shh, don't tell,
It's a dirty little secret,
It's only for you to know.

You should be ashamed of yourself
You should have listened
It's your fault now.
Afterall,
You didn't listen to the rules.

Texted a boy when you shouldn't have,
Shh, don't talk about it.
He only wanted to talk about
Sex,
Your body, his candy
Now, what would make you hotter?
Sexier?
More appealing?
But Shh, don't tell.

It's a big secret I'm told.
To keep inside for ages.
But if I write it here
For all to see.
It's not a secret anymore.

Is it?

So dear Reader,
Shh, don't tell.

Freedom

Freedom is an idea,
Not something tangible,
Something we can hold,
In the palm of our hands,
Freedom can't tickle our cheeks,
Like a feather.

It is curious though,
How everyone yearns for it,
In one way or another.

I've come to learn,
People enjoy the material,
Why do we give gifts,
If not for this fact?

You can't gift freedom,
Maybe that's why,
It's so sought for.

Some claim to hold freedom,
Yet they want for more,
How come this is so?

Is it the same greed?
The same that seeks gold,
When there's already piles stowed?
Always wanting more.

All people see is a cage,
A make believe one to be sure,
But to the captive?
It is as real as the sun.

Captive shouts "freedom!"
But his cage is faux,
He can't tell what he has already won.

The outside has nothing left, to give,
For there is no such thing,
As a make believe key,
For a make believe cage.

Unless of course,
You are the captive.

Broken

Does it hurt you too?
We share the same space,
Talk to the same people,
Go to the same parties.
No talking,
No looking,
No awkward gab,
No.

You keep staring.
Do you miss me?
Do you know you broke me?
Your words the final straw,
I was struggling.
It's why you left,
Isn't it?
I scared you,
I scared myself.
You didn't want to deal with my pain.
The cutting, bruising,
Screaming, crying.

You knew every inch of my mind.
I let you in,
I let myself trust you.

But you left.
Traitor.

But tell me,
Why would I still risk it all for Traitor?
I'd give my life for theirs,
No hesitation,
Traitor broke me,
I save them in return.
Is that how this works?

Traitor demands,
"Give everything you have to me"
I obey.
I cry as Traitor takes all the pieces of me.

Why do you treat me this way?
Taking, never giving
Please stop.
I have no more to give.
Everything falling apart.
Everything is broken.
You laugh and spit.
I cry on my knees,
And pray to God,
Please take this away.

But I can't live without you.
Can't live without your laugh,
Your smile,
You.

Letters Lost to Sea Pt 2

I write to you
because I need someone to listen to me.
Believe the words I write,
listen and not laugh in mocking
at my ambitions and hopes for the future.

Fear for me when I say
I am writing at night,
in a white glowing gown,
where the wolves groan and moan
in hunger,
with a lantern by my side on uneven ground,
sitting on flammable moss.

Yes, fear for me.
For this is the situation
I have placed myself in now.
On purpose.

Maybe that is what's wrong with me.
I am too attracted to danger.
Hence, my current situation,
And this letter.

You see,

One Who Listens,
I've always believed
Something is wrong with me.
Maybe of my own doing.
For what God would make
a creature like me,
with an achingly beautiful longing inside
to leave The House.

At least,
it would be beautiful
if life was like the poetry I read in my books.
Instead it pulls with the knives it carries.
Longing can be a vicious thing,
Don't you agree?

The House Pt 1

The photocopy house sits in the corner of my
mind,
Mind palace,
Roman room,
Palace of memories.
It has many names.

It's bright and organized,
Comforting.
There's darkness too,
It's not all bright and happy.
Nothing is.

Nearly every house has a backyard,
Mine does too.
Don't tell anyone,
But the house is broken,
Like me.

There's a hole,
Shh, don't tell.
Do you wanna know what it holds?
There're my nightmares,
My arms shattered into pieces,
My birth father,

Never here in life, there in my mind.

There's a hole in the back of my mind,
I put all the bad things there.
Maybe if I bury them they'll leave me alone.

My Love Fog and Sea

She is the mist and fog
She rolls over the sea
With her eccentric wills and wyles
Diseased with the ideas from shores the oceans
cannot reach.

Her tendrils wrap and drape around the sea
And pulls her into a idle dance
Against the violas of ghosts.

She smells of ink and parchment,
Writing with stylograph and paint
To channel the old poets of time,
Her hair of fresh roses and dew mornings.
Her hands decorated sailors,
Experienced in my formidable waves.

Letters Lost to Sea Pt 3

The House is what keeps us safe.
I know this.
The world knows this.
But I wish it wasn't true.
Our world is small,
One Who Listens.
I've already explored
every cranny and nook and keyhole.
Already lived
every conquest
every adventure
every side quest here.
Nothing I've done
so far
has squelched
the adventurousness inside.
Maybe writing to you will help.
Sincerely,
The One Who Writes

The House Pt 2

The One Who Writes,
The One Who Listens,
Those Who Shall Not Be Named,
They live here.
In this house.
They can't escape.
I won't let them.

The Voices

There are voices whispering and shouting in my
ear
the grim reaper behind the teacher.
I want it all to stop.
The voices.
So I could focus.
There are more coming; growing.
The panic is rising in my chest
I don't know how to ask for help.
I want it all to stop.

I couldn't disrupt the class.

It's not my fault.
I didn't ask to be like this.
I can't ask for help,
that would turn into a yell,
a shout,
a scream.
That would disrupt the class.
I'd get in trouble, kicked out.

My thoughts are spiraling, I just want it all to
stop.
Make it stop.

Leave me be,
Let me have peace.
Isn't that a basic human right?
To be at peace?
But the voices and the ghosts.
They're in my ear and the room and behind me
and in front of me and
Why won't they leave me alone?

I raise my hand
"Can I go to the nurse?"
"The nurses can't help you"
"The others can see the crazy"
"It's written on your forehead can't you see?"
"You stupid creature"
"You're a disruption"
I wish the voices would shut up.

The grim reaper follows me
He stands with me by the nurse
"He'll hurt you"
"Don't trust the nurse"
"The pills are poison"
"Don't trust, not trust"

"You got sent home, now look at what you've
done!"
I take the pills my mother gives me

Despite the voices.
"You're poisoning your body,"
I'm used to the voices by now
But that doesn't make them less scary
I wish it did.

Sometimes I wish,
No, most of the time I wish,
No, all the time I wish,
I could hide from my mind.
In the darkest corners of the globe
Where it can't find me.
Where it doesn't tell me I'm crazy
Where it doesn't say I'm going mad.
Where I can just be.

I don't remember anything else,
Sorry.

The Not-Crazy woman's mantra

I'm not crazy
I'm not crazy
I'm not crazy

I swear I'm not crazy.

The Cycle

I got stuff to do.
I don't want to get up,
There are things that need to get done.
My legs don't want to work.

I should probably eat.
I don't want to eat.
Did I really gain so much weight?
Maybe I'll take along
Something small.

I don't want to be here,
I don't want to be here,
I don't want to be here.
I need to be here.
I don't have a choice.

I'd rather be in bed,
Sleeping the day away.
But I can't,
There are people who depend on me.
So I brush myself aside,
And I get to work.

The House Pt 3

There are symbols in my house,
The devil in the corner,
 is the number six,
The number six is a parking space.
Daddy asked me to remember where we parked,
You ask when?
Three years ago of course.

There's two men
Two men wearing three piece suits,
Drinking tea
The Two Gentlemen of Verona.
Leftover from the challenge,
Memorize Shakespeare plays in order.

But what's leftover in the basement
That's my favorite room,
It's the most interesting.
There lies Shakespeare,
There lies the chess table,
It's pieces lined up in neat rows.

Did you know Shakespeare's my friend?
He sits and talks with me.
Don't be scared,

It's not really him,
Of course.
It's all up here,
In my head.

Daily Reminders

Just keep going,
It'll get better,
Don't compare yourself,
Everyone's journey is different,
You're good enough,
You're struggles don't define you,
No matter how much you tell yourself,
They do.
I know it's hard,
Really I do,
These poems,
My story,
I've been through hell,
I made it through,
I know you can to.